Today God
Wants You to
Know. . .

*You Have
Purpose*

Sherry L. Worel

BARBOUR BOOKS
An Imprint of Barbour Publishing, Inc.

ISBN 978-1-64352-264-7

Published by Barbour Books, an imprint of Barbour Publishing, Inc., 1810 Barbour Drive, Uhrichsville, Ohio 44683, www.barbourbooks.com

Our mission is to inspire the world with the life-changing message of the Bible.

Member of the
Evangelical Christian
Publishers Association

Printed in the United States of America.

CONTENTS

Introduction

*"For the LORD of hosts has planned,
and who can frustrate it?"*
ISAIAH 14:27 NASB

God has a plan and a purpose for each of His kids. Because He is a good God and a good Father, those plans ultimately work for our good. In Christ, we have worth, dignity, and significance. We matter and everything we do matters. Sometimes His purposes are hidden or difficult to accomplish. Sometimes the circumstances of life obscure His face. But as we seek His will in His Word, there is peace for today and heaven awaiting tomorrow. We pray you will find encouragement from God in these pages—to live in the love of a Father who values and cherishes you and gives your life purpose.

OUR LIVES HAVE MEANING AND VALUE

He Saved Us

*He saved us, not because of righteous things
we had done, but because of his mercy.*

TITUS 3:5 NIV

There is a difference between God's mercy (not receiving the condemnation we deserve) and His grace (receiving the blessings we do not deserve). Our best efforts are described in grotesque fashion in Isaiah 64:6. We deserve the wrath of God, but because of His mercy (literally, His compassion) we are saved. That reality gives enormous direction to our lives. As the old hymn says, "Saved, how I love to proclaim it, saved by the blood of the Lamb, His child and forever I am!"

Fearfully and Wonderfully Made

I will praise thee; for I am fearfully and wonderfully made: marvellous are thy works.

PSALM 139:14 KJV

From time to time, most of us complain about our bodies. Maybe our nose is too long, our eyes too round, and our mouth too wide. We forget that God's master plan specifically included our features. When the psalmist suggests that we were "fearfully made," he is telling us to consider our bodies with a kind of reverence. We are looking at God's handiwork. And He made no mistakes, so maybe we should complain less and praise more.

It Has Already Been Given to Us

Everything that goes into a life of pleasing God has been miraculously given to us by getting to know, personally and intimately, the One who invited us to God.

2 Peter 1:3 MSG

Stop the struggle. We have already been given all that we need for this life and the one to come. Christ has arranged for it all. Our job is to stay connected to Him—through prayer, meditation, and Bible reading. We see His face as we serve. We already have all the tools necessary to accomplish His will in our lives. We just need to use them.

We Have Great Dignity

*For as the heavens are higher than the earth,
so are my ways higher than your ways, and my
thoughts than your thoughts.*

ISAIAH 55:9 KJV

God's "ways" (operational principles) are "higher" than ours. The Hebrew term means "to be exalted," and it refers to people or things of high or great dignity. God has a plan for us, and in it we have great worth. Left to our own devices, we will muddle through life making little spiritual progress. But once we realize that His way is superior, we have value and dignity. What a great thought to start the day with!

You Are Valuable

"So do not fear; you are more valuable than many sparrows."

MATTHEW 10:31 NASB

A sparrow is a small brown or gray bird that feeds on seeds and tiny insects and is found in great numbers around Israel. They have little value, but Jesus said that one of them could not fall to the ground without the heavenly Father knowing about it. And then He goes on to say that we are "more valuable" than those sparrows. In Greek that phrase carries the idea of superior worth. What is worth more than the constant attention of God Almighty? Wow, we are valuable!

Set Apart

"Before I formed you in the womb I knew you,
before you were born I set you apart."

JEREMIAH 1:5 NIV

"To be set apart" carries the idea of being "ordained." The Hebrew word is used about 2,000 times in the Old Testament and means to be "literally placed." In the same way, God set the stars in the sky (Genesis 1:17) and a rainbow in the clouds (Genesis 9:13); He has literally placed us on a course before we were even born. Being set aside for a very specific purpose is a goal worth pursuing.

God Has Plans

"I have it all planned out—plans to take care of you, not abandon you, plans to give you the future you hope for."

Jeremiah 29:11 MSG

In Hebrew, the phrase "the future you hope for" originally referred to a bright red cord like the one Rahab used in her window to save her family. Jeremiah uses that same symbolism to send Israel's deported leaders a message of hope and encouragement. Just as God promised Israel an expected end, He promises us a future that He controls. Watch for it.

Worked into Something Good

*That's why we can be so sure that every
detail in our lives of love for God is
worked into something good.*

Romans 8:28 MSG

Paul chose a very specific Greek word to
convey the idea that the details of our lives
(the good, the bad, and the ugly) all "work
together" for our benefit. We get the English
word *synergism* from this term. It means that
all those details or circumstances cooperate
or contribute toward God's stated goal. We
certainly do not always understand what
is being accomplished. But we can have
confidence that it is being worked into
something good.

Guided by His Eye

*I will instruct thee and teach thee in
the way which thou shalt go: I will
guide thee with mine eye.*

PSALM 32:8 KJV

As children, we all knew what it was like to
be directed by our parents via one of those
"looks." In a similar way, the psalmist is letting
us know that God is actively guiding our lives
and He is doing so with His eyes. Literally, it
means that He is giving us silent counsel or
advice. He is accomplishing His plans, guiding
us through the circumstances of life, and His
plans will never fail. Check out His eyes!

He Controls the End

*I will cry unto God most high; unto God
that performeth all things for me.*

PSALM 57:2 KJV

God performs all things for me. In Hebrew, it
is the idea of bringing something to an end,
to complete it. He perfects all things and
sees that they accomplish His will. We are not
robots, but we are sovereignly directed toward
an expected or anticipated end. We do not
need to thrash around wondering what all the
details of life add up to; He knows. We cry out
and He performs His will. How comforting is
that?

Changed

*And we all, who with unveiled faces
contemplate the Lord's glory, are being
transformed into his image.*

2 CORINTHIANS 3:18 NIV

"Are being transformed": this is the Greek word *metamorphosis*. It's a change of condition. Not because of anything we have done, but by His grace we are being formed into His image. We have great worth because we are slowly becoming like Him. Think butterfly. The invisible process of spiritual transformation is at work. Changed for a purpose!

We Are God's Kids

*We are His people and
the sheep of His pasture.*
PSALM 100:3 NASB

The Beatles struck a chord when they sang,
"All the lonely people, where do they all come
from? All the lonely people, where do they all
belong?" A sense of belonging is absolutely
crucial to everyone's health and well-being.
We need to have an emotional "home."
The psalmist addresses that basic need and
assures us that we are God's. We belong to
Him and "live and move and have our being"
(Acts 17:28 NIV) in His pasture. Such comfort!

We Belong to Him

"Behold, all souls are Mine; the soul of the father as well as the soul of the son is Mine."

EZEKIEL 18:4 NASB

Nothing about us came by chance. Every woman has a distinct personality, exclusive fingerprints, and unique DNA markers. Where did all that uniqueness come from? We get the answer in Thornton Wilder's three-act play, *Our Town*. One of the characters in that play signs her address like this: "I live in Grover's Corner, New Hampshire, United States of America, Western Hemisphere, Planet Earth, Solar System, The Universe, and The Mind of God." We belong to Him!

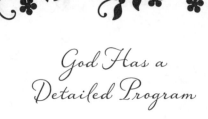

God Has a Detailed Program

*I will exalt You, I will give thanks to Your name;
for You have worked wonders, plans formed
long ago, with perfect faithfulness.*

ISAIAH 25:1 NASB

Hannibal Smith (from the TV series *The A-Team*) often said that he loved it when a plan came together. So do we. We want to know that all the circumstances of life have meaning, that they are part of a grand scheme. Isaiah affirms God's plans and remarks that they were formed long ago. There is amazing comfort in knowing God considered our lives a very long time ago. Clearly, He is in control.

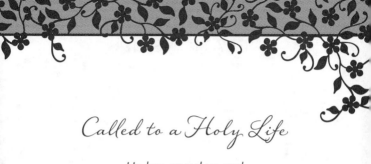

Called to a Holy Life

He has saved us and
call us to a holy life.
2 TIMOTHY 1:9 NIV

God has saved us by His grace and for His own purposes. Once saved, we are called to a different kind of life. We no longer control our activities or future. To be holy does not convey moral perfection. A holy life is one set aside for specific reasons. It is to be consecrated for a virtuous cause. We no longer call the shots; He directs our lives toward a specific service.

RELATIONSHIPS

Instructing Our Children

*Write these commandments that I've given
you today on your hearts. Get them inside of
you and then get them inside your children.*

DEUTERONOMY 6:6–7 MSG

Susanna Wesley was an English pastor's wife
with nineteen children. Her sons John and
Charles became notable Christian leaders of
the Methodist church. Through them, Susanna
gained an amazing spiritual legacy. And she
did it by taking personal time each week with
each child. On Mondays she met with Molly,
Tuesdays with Hetty, Wednesdays with Nancy,
and so on. Her time with the children was
intentional, steeped in scripture, and directed
to Christ. How's your instruction time with
your kids?

Praying for Your Children

The fear of the LORD is the beginning of wisdom, and the knowledge of the Holy One is understanding.

PROVERBS 9:10 NASB

We should be confident that the Lord loves hearing mothers praying scripture with their children in mind. This verse in Proverbs might be paraphrased, "Lord, teach my children to fear You, since this is the beginning of wisdom. Add years to their lives as they learn to have Your perspective on any situation." There are hundreds of passages like this that can be used to pray on behalf of our children. It's powerful. Try it today.

Caring for Grandchildren

*May you live to see
your children's children.*
PSALM 128:6 NIV

Having grandchildren is one of life's greatest joys. And having them live with you is a special blessing. It can be a great deal of work, but what a privilege to be so involved with those little ones. Let's treasure our time with them. Let's make a significant investment in them as we talk and share our life experiences. It is a treat to be spiritual role models. So as we stick godly fingerprints all over their souls, let's faithfully pray for them.

Strengthen the Hand of a Friend

And Jonathan Saul's son arose,
and went to David into the wood,
and strengthened his hand in God.
1 SAMUEL 23:16 KJV

When you "strengthen someone's hand," you encourage them. You speak words of affirmation; you remind them of God's faithfulness and you urge them to immerse themselves in His grace. This Hebrew phrase carries the idea of directing someone to be courageous in spite of their circumstances. Like Jonathan, we all have friends who need to be encouraged. Look around. Whose hand can you strengthen today?

Love Others Like You Love Yourself

You do well when you complete
the Royal Rule of the Scriptures:
"Love others as you love yourself."
JAMES 2:8 MSG

We all know how to love and dote on ourselves. But if we want to fulfill God's grand plan for our lives, we need to follow the Royal Rule and consider the needs of others. We need to give generously (not just when we deem someone worthy). We need to forgive (even when we were clearly wronged). We need to avoid gossip and slander (speaking kindly even to the mean-spirited). So who needs your love today?

Serving Our Families

First thing in the morning,
she dresses for work, rolls up
her sleeves, eager to get started.
PROVERBS 31:15 MSG

We often joke that a mother's work is never done, and it's true. There is an endless pile of laundry, a recurring clamor for meals, and so it goes. There is always something to be accomplished. But it is not the long list of tasks that's laudable; it's Mom's attitude that counts. Part of God's plan for all of us is to care for our families and to do so with an enthusiastic mind-set. Are you eager for the demands of today?

It's Not Enough to Just Love God

And he has given us this command:
Anyone who loves God must also
love their brother and sister.
1 JOHN 4:21 NIV

In most homes, sibling rivalry is alive and well. And this verse could help control the bickering, but that's not its primary purpose. Actually, John is trying to underscore the truth that it's not enough to just love the Lord. We have to also love those around us. This love (*agape*) is expressed when we find our joy in blessing someone else and not ourselves. When we love the Lord, we show it by the way we treat others.

Do Good

*As we have therefore opportunity, let us
do good unto all men, especially unto
them who are of the household of faith.*
GALATIANS 6:10 KJV

Part of God's plan for our lives is the repeated
action of doing useful, beneficial things for
others. In this verse, Paul highlights the need
to bless other Christians. Doing "good" in this
sense means to provide a blessing. It could be
a meal or some money or a place to live. But
it is palpable. It's not just a promise to pray or
a sweet sentiment. It's tangible. Let's consider
what good we can do today.

Cherishing Our Friends

Do not forsake your own friend.
PROVERBS 27:10 NASB

When Aristotle said that friendship is a single soul in two bodies, he must have had women in mind. Experiencing life with a dear best friend is an incredible blessing. They stimulate us and encourage us. They are like a mirror; we see ourselves in a clearer way when we spend time with them. They remind us of God's faithfulness and provide support, all the while loving us unconditionally. Cherish that special friend. Give her a call right now and tell her, "I thank my God upon every remembrance of you. . . ."

Devoted to One Another

*Be devoted to one
another in brotherly love.*
ROMANS 12:10 NASB

When an elephant is under duress, another elephant will stick its trunk in the sad one's mouth. It's a touch that seems to say, "I am here to help you." And still another elephant will start a chirping noise that seems to convey, "You don't have to go through this alone." Animal behavior is so instructive. Paul was equally instructive when he told the Romans to be devoted to one another. This devotion is a kind of affection that can be seen by others. Who needs to hear you chirp today?

Spiritual Footprints

*The things which you have heard from
me. . .entrust these to faithful men who
will be able to teach others also.*
2 Timothy 2:2 NASB

Recording a mother's spiritual journey is a
powerful way to influence generations to
come. Children can likely reiterate the tenets
of our personal faith, but how can we influence
grandchildren? How can we leave spiritual
footprints? One way is to write in our Bibles
and keep them for our families. Journaling will
leave a trail of faith, and so will marking up a
favorite hymnbook. Let's start thinking of ways
to make the spiritual footprints obvious.

Marriage Is Honorable

Marriage is honourable in all,
and the bed undefiled.

HEBREWS 13:4 KJV

We live in a world of throwaway commitments. One city recently proposed temporary marriage licenses as an alternative to plunging into a lifetime of faithfulness. God's plan is one woman for one man, and it is an honorable plan. We can't survive in a culture where vows mean nothing. Today is a great day to thank God for your husband and pray for him (warts and all).

Help Her

I ask you to receive her in the Lord in a way worthy of his people and to give her any help she may need from you.

ROMANS 16:2 NIV

Paul is urging this church in Rome to meet the needs of a woman named Phoebe. He chooses a specific phrase to convey the concept—"give her any help she may need." Literally, he is asking them to stand by her, to place themselves at her disposal. The thought is to figure out exactly what she needs and provide it. There are people all around who need us to stand with them. Let's find some today.

Touch Them

And they were bringing children to
Him so that He might touch them.
MARK 10:13 NASB

Women understand the power of a touch. When we are physically touched in kindness, our blood pressure goes down, endorphins are released, and we just plain feel good. Two-handed handshakes are better than one. A tousle of the hair means something. A pat on the back is much more than just an expression; it is an affirmation of a job well done. A hand on a shoulder is reassuring. Jesus touched people; so should we.

A Good Fight

"Put your minds on the Master,
great and awesome, and then fight for
your brothers, your sons, your daughters,
your wives, and your homes."

NEHEMIAH 4:14 MSG

In context, this passage has to do with a physical fight regarding the wall in Jerusalem. But there are many other situations that need our diligent response. As wives and mothers, we are the keepers of our homes, and our children deserve our persistent protection. In this electronic age, it takes effort. Moms need to fight for the purity of their children. Turn off devices. Monitor activities. Say no. Fight for the hearts of those you love. It matters.

Love One Another

"A new command I give you:
Love one another."
JOHN 13:34 NIV

C. S. Lewis once remarked, "Affection is responsible for nine-tenths of whatever solid and durable happiness there is in our lives." And he is so right. Jesus commanded us to love one another. And every mother knows it takes affection to express our love. It takes a touch, a word, a kindness, a gift of any size, a tone of voice, or a smile. If we want to be happy, really happy, we must begin today to love others.

Living Life with Others

*And Ruth said, Intreat me not to leave
thee, or to return from following after thee:
for whither thou goest, I will go; and
where thou lodgest, I will lodge.*

RUTH 1:16 KJV

This verse is often found on the inside of
wedding bands, but in context, it's a daughter-
in-law committing herself to doing life with
her mother-in-law. Ruth is promising to be
an integral part of Naomi's life. God never
intended for His kids to live the solitary life.
His plan is for us to be in a community, to
know others and to be known.

WORK IS IMPORTANT

Signing Our Work

*Slack habits and sloppy work
are as bad as vandalism.*
PROVERBS 18:9 MSG

The story goes that the night before his sculpture the *Pietà* was to be unveiled, Michelangelo overheard some critics questioning whether it was really his work. So he went back into the studio and chiseled his entire name along the fold of Mary's garment. It is important to take pride in our work whether it is in a kitchen or a boardroom. Let's make sure and sign our names to everything we do. No slack habits!

A Good Reputation

Seest thou a man diligent in his business?
he shall stand before kings.

PROVERBS 22:29 KJV

Most women appreciate having a good
reputation. We would like to be noticed by our
bosses. But how do we gain a good report?
The Bible says that we must be diligent. The
original Hebrew word emphasizes a person's
skill at their job. Before we "stand before
kings," we have to patiently learn our jobs
and then do them repetitively with excellence.
Others will notice.

Work, and We Get to Eat

*He who tills his land will have
plenty of bread, but he who pursues
worthless things lacks sense.*

PROVERBS 12:11 NASB

In Hebrew, a worthless thing is empty. It is hollow and without meaning. Too often, we avoid hard work and get distracted by all manner of silliness. This wise proverb is making a clear statement regarding employment: if you work, you get to eat. No work, no food. It's a basic but powerful motivator. Since we all like to eat, it's a good time to pause and thank the Lord for our work.

Affirming Our Work

And let the loveliness of our Lord, our God,
rest on us, confirming the work that we do.
Oh, yes. Affirm the work that we do!
PSALM 90:17 MSG

When we ask God to affirm our work, we are literally asking Him to let it stand in an upright position or be noted as steadfast. It is set in place and by extension has value and worth. It's not just something we do to pay the rent. With God's stamp of approval, our work is important and established as a meaningful pursuit.

Organization

Let all things be done
decently and in order.
1 CORINTHIANS 14:40 KJV

Although the immediate context for this verse is an organized church service, the principle applies to everything we do. Much of our purpose in life involves our work. Work that is pleasing to the Lord is "done decently" or with decorum. The original language stipulates that our work should be fashioned well. And it is accomplished in good "order," meaning it is well regulated and without confusion. No one wants to work in an environment of chaos. Have you considered that being organized is a spiritual hallmark too?

Results

Throw yourselves into the work of the Master,
confident that nothing you do for him
is a waste of time or effort.

1 CORINTHIANS 15:58 MSG

Regardless of the kind of career we have (in
the living room or a boardroom), we pray
that it matters and that our effort counts
for something. That's why Paul assured the
Corinthians that their work was not a waste
of time. The Greek term means "to be full."
When our work is done for God, it's full of
meaning, it is fruitful. So let's throw ourselves
into our jobs this week and watch Him bless
our efforts.

Satisfaction in Our Work

*A person can do nothing better
than to eat and drink and find
satisfaction in their own toil.*

ECCLESIASTES 2:24 NIV

When God included work in His plan for our
lives, He never envisioned the endless stress
that accompanies much of our modern work
world. The term *satisfaction* in this verse
implies rest or the ability to lay something
down and walk away. When we work with the
right attitude and for the right reasons, it just
feels good, and we can walk away with a real
sense of godly accomplishment.

A Mind to Work

So we built the wall and the whole wall
was joined together to half its height,
for the people had a mind to work.

NEHEMIAH 4:6 NASB

Negative people poison the workplace. Positive, encouraging workers, on the other hand, ignite one another's efforts. Creativity flows, energy multiplies, and they produce results. So it was with the wall in Jerusalem. People had "a mind to work." Literally, they had the will to focus on the job at hand. They ignored the critical voices and got after it. Attitude mattered then and it matters now. Do you have a mind to work today?

Our Obedience Affects Our Work

The LORD will send a blessing on your barns and on everything you put your hand to.
DEUTERONOMY 28:8 NIV

This passage begins in verses 1–2 with the statement that "If you fully obey the LORD. . . . All these blessings will come on you." There is a direct correlation between our character and God's blessing on our work. We can't expect to prosper when our hearts are not attuned to Him. That blessing we seek is a form of God's favor on the righteous. So, before you head off to work, check your heart, and then seek that blessing.

Committing Our Work to God

*Commit thy works unto the LORD,
and thy thoughts shall be established.*

PROVERBS 16:3 KJV

The root idea of the Hebrew word for *commit* means "to roll." When someone's work was "rolled" to God, it was committed or entrusted to Him. It is a way to say, "Lord, here are my efforts for today. I give them to You to bless." And when we do that, our minds are settled, our thoughts are focused. We are working out a part of His plan, and it feels good.

Your Business Is His Business

*A just weight and balance are the LORD's:
all the weights of the bag are his work.*
PROVERBS 16:11 KJV

In scripture, weights and other forms of
measurement were the basis of commerce.
A merchant's honesty was reflected by which
weights he used. A wicked scale or a bag
of deceptive weights (Micah 6:11) marked a
seller as a cheat. And so it is today. Although
not many of us are literally using weights,
honesty still matters. Our word is a bond. How
we conduct business reflects on our Savior.
Our business is His business.

Providing for Our Family

*But if anyone does not provide for
his own, and especially for those of
his household, he has denied the faith
and is worse than an unbeliever.*

1 TIMOTHY 5:8 NASB

Work occupies about 40 percent of our waking lives. As a required activity for all adults, many see it as a necessary evil. But here Paul seems to elevate our labor (mental or physical) to an activity of faith. Our very belief system urges us to work hard and care for our families. Think about it. Our work shouldn't be a drudgery; it is a part of God's purposeful design.

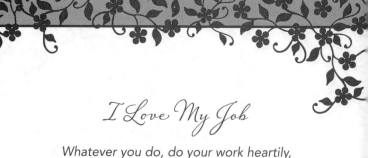

I Love My Job

Whatever you do, do your work heartily,
as for the Lord rather than for men.
COLOSSIANS 3:23 NASB

Instead of taking careful notes, a court reporter sat for months typing "I hate my job" over and over again. Needless to say, once he was caught, it totally disrupted the flow of legal proceedings, and cases had to be retried. We might not be actually typing that sentiment, but women may be silently mouthing, "I hate my job," too. Paul wanted to encourage us all to see our work as a kind of worship unto the Lord. So try it. . . . "I love my job, I love my job."

Today's Schedule

Whatever you do,
do it all for the glory of God.
1 CORINTHIANS 10:31 NIV

In *Alice in Wonderland*, Alice asks the Cheshire Cat for advice: "Which road should I take?" The Cat replies, "Where are you going?" Alice says she doesn't know, and the Cat replies, "If you don't know where you are going, any road will get you there." Any old road doesn't work for God's daughters. Let's look at our schedules for today and choose those things that lead to His glory.

Sincerity

*"My words come from an upright heart;
my lips sincerely speak what I know."*
JOB 33:3 NIV

When a mediocre chiseler makes a mistake
in a statue, he might just smear some hot
wax into the crack and pass it off as "good
enough." The Latin term for not using wax is
sine cere, from which we get the English word
sincere. To speak sincerely is to be known
as trustworthy. At home or in the office, let's
make sure our words today are not just passed
off with a "bit of wax." Let's be known as
workers who have an upright heart.

SERVICE COUNTS

He Won't Forget

For God is not unrighteous to forget
your work and labour of love.
HEBREWS 6:10 KJV

Often God's purpose for our lives is displayed in the way we serve others. In this verse, Paul uses two different Greek words (in English, *work* and *labor*) to convey the importance of our service. Interestingly, the term *work* comes from a root meaning "to wail or beat our breasts" in emotion. This is a service or labor that really matters to us. We are not serving out of some kind of obligation. We want to reach out and help. And God will not forget that effort.

Every Day

*And he said to them all, If any man will come
after me, let him deny himself, and take
up his cross daily, and follow me.*

LUKE 9:23 KJV

The need to serve others as part of God's plan
is a relentless pursuit. It is a daily demand.
We don't get to take a day off or choose to
ignore a need because we are having a tough
day. God provides every day (1 Chronicles
16), and we need to encourage others every
day (Hebrews 3:13). Maybe the words *follow
Him* ought to be the top line of our schedules
EVERY DAY.

Salt

"Let me tell you why you are here. You're here to be salt-seasoning that brings out the God-flavors of this earth. If you lose your saltiness, how will people taste godliness?"
MATTHEW 5:13 MSG

Jesus knew salt is an essential seasoning for food from all cultures. It is important for food preservation and cooking. So He used salt as an illustration saying that it is our job to bring God-flavoring to the world. Without our active participation in service to others, no one gets to "taste and see that the LORD is good" (Psalm 34:8 KJV). So, get out of the shaker and into the world!

Our Sacrifice

Therefore I urge you, brethren, by the mercies of God, to present your bodies a living and holy sacrifice, acceptable to God, which is your spiritual service of worship.

ROMANS 12:1 NASB

The Israelites demonstrated their devotion to God by bringing animal sacrifices to the temple. It was their way of worshipping. Today, we do not offer up bulls or goats; instead, we bring ourselves to the Father. Spiritually, we bring our physical bodies to God and offer them as a sacrifice. In essence we say, "Here I am; use me for Your glory." How will He use you today?

Throw a Party

Serve the LORD with gladness.
PSALM 100:2 KJV

We serve the Lord when we serve others. The psalmist set the tone for that service when he wrote this song. That word *gladness* in Hebrew reflects the activities associated with the feast days of Israel or a wedding celebration. If we were translating it today, we might say something like: "Let's throw a party and serve the Lord!" Truth is, serving our neighbors or coworkers shouldn't be a chore. Done with the right attitude, it's a celebration!

Work with a Smile on Your Face

*Don't just do what you have to do to get
by, but work heartily, as Christ's servants
doing what God wants you to do.
And work with a smile on your face.*
EPHESIANS 6:7 MSG

Once we settle that our everyday tasks are
part of God's plan, our projects for our families
or friends should become easier. Attitude is
the key to our service. A smile on our face is
a window to our heart. It says, "I care about
you and this project. I am happy to help. I am
motivated by my relationship with the Lord.
Bring it on!"

Serve One Another

By love serve one another.
GALATIANS 5:13 KJV

In the context of teaching on spiritual freedom, Paul makes the grand statement that encapsulates all of the Christian life: serve one another. And he uses a term for serve that directly reflects the life of a slave. It literally means "act like a slave to everyone around you." Volunteer to put their needs above your own. Do what needs to be done, and do it selflessly. It is a tough command that can't be ignored if we want to follow God's plan for our lives.

His Work

*He creates each of us by Christ Jesus
to join him in the work he does, the good
work he has gotten ready for us to do,
work we had better be doing.*
EPHESIANS 2:10 MSG

Sometimes as moms, we gather all the supplies necessary to do a cooking project before our kids show up in the kitchen. We get the work ready for them. So does the Lord. He prepares the situation and then invites us to come join in the work. Let's look around. What has He prepared for you today?

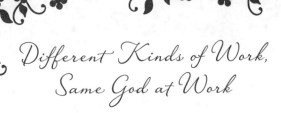

Different Kinds of Work, Same God at Work

*There are different kinds of service,
but the same Lord. There are different
kinds of working, but in all of them and
in everyone it is the same God at work.*

1 CORINTHIANS 12:5–6 NIV

We women are notorious for comparing ourselves with others. We compare our looks, our families, and our skill sets. But Paul wanted to make sure the Corinthians realized that no one's service was more important than anyone else's. Our spiritual jobs might be diverse. We might have different gifts and abilities. But ultimately we all work under the supervision of the same Lord. No reason to compare!

Put Pockets

For unto whomsoever much is given,
of him shall be much required.
LUKE 12:48 KJV

Awhile back, it seems that England was inundated with pickpockets. Some Londoners wanted to protect their international reputation as a friendly city so they organized themselves and began putting money *into* visitors' pockets. *Time* magazine called these generous people "put pockets." It seems that these folks stumbled onto an important spiritual principle. It goes like this: If you have, then give. So, would you like to be a put pocket? Whom can you bless today?

Dealing with Depression

*"And if you give yourself to the hungry
and satisfy the desire of the afflicted,
then your light will rise in darkness and
your gloom will become like midday."*

ISAIAH 58:10 NASB

The prophet Isaiah seemed to understand that one of the best ways to deal with depression is to get active and involve yourself in someone else's life. The Hebrew word for *gloom* means a kind of darkness. It makes life obscure. But when we feed the hungry or help the sick, our world brightens and our energy level soars. Reaching out in service turns on the light for all of us.

The Folks with the Cardboard Signs

"You shall not harden your heart, nor close your hand from your poor brother; but you shall freely open your hand to him."

DEUTERONOMY 15:7–8 NASB

We have all driven by the folks on the side of the road holding up cardboard signs. Too often we instinctively start an analysis of whether they really need our help. We check out their shoes, look for labels on their jeans, anything that can disqualify them from asking for some money. But take another look at Moses' instruction: Do not "harden your heart." Do not "close your hand." Maybe we need a different mind-set.

Orphans and Widows

*Religion that God our Father accepts as
pure and faultless is this: to look after
orphans and widows in their distress.*

JAMES 1:27 NIV

James understood that religion is much more
than a spiritual organization; it is an activity. It
is an activity addressing the weakest among
us. He used a Greek word to signify that these
folks are being crushed and squeezed by the
circumstances of their lives. Children without
parents, single elderly women, and others
compressed by their lot in life need relief. How
can we provide some help today?

We Have Everything We Need

His divine power has given us
everything we need for a godly life.
2 PETER 1:3 NIV

Before we start a project, we need to make sure we have all the materials at hand. There is nothing more frustrating than being halfway through a recipe and realizing you don't have the correct spice. But in life, God has made certain that we have everything we need to serve others. Our personality, our spiritual gift set, our life circumstances perfectly match the work at hand. All excuses are gone. Whom do you need to serve today?

In Order to Serve, We Need to Be Able to See

*"For God sees not as man sees,
for man looks at the outward appearance,
but the LORD looks at the heart."*
1 SAMUEL 16:7 NASB

As if women can't be catty enough on our own, there are now apps on our phones that can rate the attractiveness of women around us. These apps scan a person's face and, using optimal measurements, instantly rate that person's attractiveness. The developers claim it's all in good fun. But it's just another way to evaluate people on the basis of their looks. Let's stop that and learn to see others as God sees them.

OUR ETERNITY IS SECURE

We Can Know for Sure

*These things have I written unto you that
believe on the name of the Son of God;
that ye may know that ye have eternal life.*
1 JOHN 5:13 KJV

When asked, "Do you know if you are going
to heaven?" folks often answer, "Well, I hope
so." But we who put our faith in Christ do not
need to just hope for our place in heaven. We
can know. John uses a word here that means
to know intuitively. It suggests a fullness of
knowledge without a modicum of doubt.
Because of Christ, heaven is our eternal
destiny. We can rest in that certainty.

He Knows Us

*Nevertheless the foundation of God
standeth sure, having this seal,
The Lord knoweth them that are his.*
2 TIMOTHY 2:19 KJV

There are several Greek words in the New Testament that are translated "to know." In this verse, *knoweth* means "to know experientially." It conveys the idea that God knows us because we have spent time together. And He knows us completely. Paul is reminding Timothy that Christ really knows us, and because of that personal attention, our eternal destiny is sealed.

Encourage One Another

*And then there will be one huge family
reunion with the Master. So reassure
one another with these words.*
1 THESSALONIANS 4:17–18 MSG

The Chicago preacher D. L. Moody once
encouraged his congregation by remarking,
"Soon you will read in the newspaper that
I am dead. Don't believe it for a moment. I
will be more alive than ever before." That is
what Paul is asserting in this verse. There is a
great family reunion coming, and we ought to
regularly remind one another of that fact. Go
encourage a friend.

His Counsel Stands

Declaring the end from the beginning,
and from ancient times the things that are
not yet done, saying, My counsel shall stand,
and I will do all my pleasure.

ISAIAH 46:10 KJV

God said it, case closed. His counsel (His words, His law, His promises) has been given and can now be leaned upon. In Hebrew, when a person's words stand, it means that they are final. The case is closed. Discussion over. As part of His plan for us, God has secured our eternal home. We can have a quiet confidence in that fact.

He Is Preparing a Place for Us

*"If I go and prepare a place for you,
I will come again and receive you to Myself,
that where I am, there you may be also."*

JOHN 14:3 NASB

When a king in the ancient Near East traveled toward home, special servants were dispatched in order to get things ready. The lodging was prepped, meals were made, and hospitality was arranged. They *prepared* for the arrival of someone important. John uses this same term to convince us that Christ has gone before us to prepare our eternal home. And He is coming back for us. Bank on it.

Sealed with a Promise

Having also believed, you were sealed in Him with the Holy Spirit of promise.
EPHESIANS 1:13 NASB

The first fourteen verses of Ephesians chapter 1 comprise the longest run-on sentence in the Greek New Testament. Paul just can't seem to contain his excitement as he lists the things God has done for us. He blessed us with every spiritual blessing. . .He predestined us to adoption. . .He redeemed us. . .He forgave us. . .and He sealed our eternal destiny by the Holy Spirit of promise. It is a done deal. Because of Christ, our eternity is secure!

A Better Country

For those who say such things make it clear that they are seeking a country of their own.
HEBREWS 11:14 NASB

Hebrews chapter 11 extols the virtues of the heroes of the faith. The writer mentions the patriarchs by name and then acknowledges those nameless saints who died as pilgrims on earth. And he sums up his thoughts by declaring that they all are waiting for a country of their own, a more preferred place to call home. That is what heaven is for the child of God—home. Rooted in His plan for us is a heavenly place of rest. Are you ready to go?

Full Warranty

God's gifts and God's call are under full warranty—
never canceled, never rescinded.

ROMANS 11:29 MSG

There is nothing worse than trying to return
something to a store that does not want to
honor its warranties. God is not like that.
What He says stands. His offer of salvation
through the sacrifice of His Son will never be
rescinded. His purposeful provision of eternal
life for His kids will never be cancelled. We can
count on it. Rest in it today.

We Are Under Guard

*For I know whom I have believed and I
am convinced that He is able to guard what
I have entrusted to Him until that day.*
2 TIMOTHY 1:12 NASB

When children hand a treasure to Mom for
safekeeping, they are convinced that she will
protect it. So it is with a child of God. When
we are confident of His plan for our lives, it is
easy to entrust Him with our very souls. We
can be confident that He will guard them until
His return.

Secure in His Hand

And I give unto them eternal life;
and they shall never perish, neither shall
any man pluck them out of my hand.
JOHN 10:28 KJV

Here is a statement of purpose (we have eternal life), bound in a statement of protection (we shall never perish). Our eternal destiny is settled because we are secure in God's hand. There is something special about a father's hand, big enough to hold what's important and strong enough to protect it. Let's be grateful today for our place in His palm.

He Chose Us

*That ye may eat and drink at
my table in my kingdom.*
LUKE 22:30 KJV

Think about all the statesmen, historical figures,
celebrities, or biblical heroes who might consider inviting you to dinner. (We can dream,
can't we?) What invitation would wow you the
most? The truth is, we have already been given
the invitation of all time. Jesus, the Son of God,
has asked us to sit at His table. Not because
we deserve it. Not because we are something
special. But because He chose us. What a
thought! What a dinner!

This Is My Story

*"Return home and tell how
much God has done for you."*
LUKE 8:39 NIV

After Jesus healed him, the demon-possessed
man began to beg for the opportunity to
travel with the Lord and His disciples. He
wanted to be part of the spiritual gang, but
Jesus had a more important job for him. He
had a personal story to tell, and it needed to
be shared. Each of us has a unique platform
from which to tell our own story. Our eternal
destiny is secure; let's share the news.

What Are We Focused On?

*Set your affection on things above,
not on things on the earth.*
COLOSSIANS 3:2 KJV

To "set your affection" on something implies a real search or quest. Paul used a Greek term here that denotes a serious, active, and single-minded pursuit of something important. He is urging us to fix our spiritual eyes on heaven and not on the everyday details of this life. We are admonished to be heavenly minded. We are to strain, as it were, toward something much more valuable. What are you focused on today?

Wait for It

Live self-controlled, upright and godly
lives in this present age, while we
wait for the blessed hope.
TITUS 2:12–13 NIV

We women spend at least a half hour a day waiting. Over the course of our lives we spend 270 days just waiting in lines or in traffic or for the sandman. But Paul was encouraging another kind of waiting in this verse. It is an expectant and confident wait. With patience, we look forward to the blessed hope of Christ's return. That mind-set is a great way to start the day!

Not Home Yet

Instead, they were longing for a
better country—a heavenly one.
HEBREWS 11:16 NIV

C. S. Lewis remarked, "If I find in myself a
desire which no experience in this world can
satisfy, the most probable explanation is that
I was made for another world." Or as the
old hymn says, "This world is not my home,
I'm just a-passing through." As wives and
mothers, it often falls to us to make a house
a home. But if we sink our roots too deep
into this world, we won't long for the next.
Go ahead, review Revelation 22 and remind
yourself what it's going to be like!

THERE ARE NO ACCIDENTS IN LIFE

There Are No Accidents

Even then God had designs on me.
Why, when I was still in my mother's womb he
chose and called me out of sheer generosity!
GALATIANS 1:15 MSG

The events of our lives are not random. We are not just bouncing through life rebounding off various encounters and aimlessly wandering around. God has a plan for us. We have purpose and direction. Paul told the Galatians that God's grand plan began even before our birth. He picked us and gave us work to do. We are not accidents, nor are the details of our lives. Very cool!

Stages of Life

*Like an open book, you watched me grow
from conception to birth; all the stages
of my life were spread out before you.*

PSALM 139:16 MSG

If a cooking project has several steps involved,
a good chef will gather the supplies and
organize things before starting the actual
cooking process. God is like that too. Before
we were born, He laid out the various stages
of our lives and purposefully sorted them.
There are no surprises or mysteries to His plan.
All of our stages or circumstances of life are
laid out before Him. It's time to trust Him!

Part of God's Family

Though my father and mother forsake me,
the Lord will receive me.
PSALM 27:10 NIV

Norman Rockwell's famous painting, *Freedom from Want*, depicts a stereotypical American family gathered for Thanksgiving. But not all of our families look or act like that. Many adults still struggle with the scars (physical or emotional) of childhood abandonment. The psalmist understood that kind of deep heartache, and so he reminds us all that God is our Father. Regardless of how our parents behaved, the Lord will always be there for us. We truly can risk serving Him.

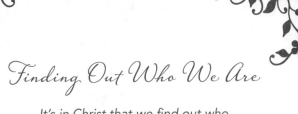

Finding Out Who We Are

*It's in Christ that we find out who
we are and what we are living for.*
EPHESIANS 1:11 MSG

The two compelling questions for all mankind
are: Who am I, and where am I going? Paul
addresses the identity issue in his letter to the
Ephesians. It is in Christ that we find out who
we are and what we are here for. Our salvation
involves so much more than just a ticket to
heaven. Identifying with Christ affirms there
are no accidents in life. We work as unto Him.
We serve our families because of Him. We are
who we are, because of Him.

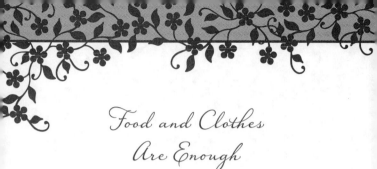

Food and Clothes Are Enough

And having food and raiment
let us be therewith content.
1 TIMOTHY 6:8 KJV

Part of the process of settling into God's plan for our lives involves an attitude adjustment. Instead of scurrying around striving for more—more anything—we must become *content*. That word implies satisfaction. Paul made it simple for his young protégé, Timothy. He told him to focus only on something to eat and something to wear. That's great advice. To be content, we have to say (and mean it), "What I have is enough."

There Is No Distinction

For there is no distinction between Jew and Greek; for the same Lord is Lord of all.

ROMANS 10:12 NASB

Human beings tend to highlight differences between races, cultures, languages, and the like. And once we have shown the differences, we establish a ranking or pecking order, and our group tends to come out on top. But Paul demolished that idea with his letter to the Roman church. Literally, he said there is "no pulling apart" or separating one group from another. God is Lord of us all. We stand before Him as one group in need of His grace—no distinctions.

The Plan of the Day

The steps of a good man are ordered by the LORD: and he delighteth in his way.

PSALM 37:23 KJV

In the military, each unit has a posted "Plan of the Day" (POD). That plan brings structure to the day's activities. So it is with the Christian's life. God has a POD for us as well. Our steps are ordered, or more literally, made firm or established. There are no accidents for God's kids. Our service is meaningful, planned out, and God gets a kick out of watching us do His will. We just need to get busy doing it!

Living in the Present

I think then that this is good in view
of the present distress, that it is
good for a man to remain as he is.
1 CORINTHIANS 7:26 NASB

Three times in this chapter, Paul urges the Corinthians to live contentedly in their present circumstance, whether married or not. That advice is good for all environments of life. Too often we are focused on getting out of a situation rather than seeing God work through the circumstances. Remaining in those moments or seasons may be His best idea. Do you need to remain where you are for a bit?

You Are Not Your Own

You are not your own; you were bought at a price.
Therefore honor God with your bodies.
1 CORINTHIANS 6:19–20 NIV

Step number one as we pursue God's plan for our lives is to recognize that God is in control. As Christians, we have been redeemed from sin and presented with a new life. We need to recognize Him for who He is and for what He does. We celebrate His goodness not only with our spirits or souls but also with our bodies. We are to honor Him physically with praise, worship, and adoration. Go ahead, move a little.

Taste and See

Taste and see that the L<small>ORD</small> is good.
P<small>SALM</small> 34:8 NIV

Every good cook understands how important
taste buds are. Each of us has between 2,000
and 8,000 of them on the surface of our
tongue. They help us recognize sour, bitter,
sweet, salty, and pleasant things. When we
taste, we are sampling and trying new things.
In this verse, the psalmist is encouraging us
to "sample" or "try on" some new aspect of
God's plan for our lives. Go ahead; reach out,
trust Him, stretch and grow a bit.

Discipline of Disturbance

He guarded him as the apple of his eye,
like an eagle that stirs up its nest and
hovers over its young, that spreads
its wings to catch them.
DEUTERONOMY 32:10–11 NIV

Often as wives and mothers struggling with
hectic schedules, we get to thinking that
God owes us a little peace. But He seems to
specialize in a kind of discipline of disturbance.
Like a mother eagle that will at the right
time forcibly shove an eaglet out of the nest,
the Lord keeps pushing His girls out of their
comfort zone and into His perfect will.

Override My Emotions

*Though the fig tree should not blossom
and there be no fruit on the vines,
though the yield of the olive should fail. . .
yet I will exult in the LORD.*
HABAKKUK 3:17–18 NASB

Just before the Babylonians devastated
Jerusalem, the prophet Habakkuk preached
a stirring message to Israel. The people were
facing deportation or worse. Emotions were
clouding their confidence in God. So he
reminded them that even with all evidence
to the contrary, God could be trusted and
praised. And He still can!

Tough Stuff

The LORD gave, and the LORD hath taken away;
blessed be the name of the LORD.

JOB 1:21 KJV

Job's children were killed. His business is
ruined. He is in great physical pain with sores
all over his body. He is depressed, and his
friends are giving lousy advice. And his spouse
thinks he should curse God and die. His tough
stuff, or things like it, might be happening
in your home too. Let's just be reminded
of God's sovereignty and declare with Job,
"Blessed be the name of the Lord."

One Word

Don't shoot off your mouth.
ECCLESIASTES 5:2 MSG

Everyone loves to make resolutions, set goals, or outline bucket lists. But maybe we should focus on just one word at a time. Less is more. With a little introspection, let's identify what kind of person we really want to become and then ask the Lord for just one word that represents that "new" you. Meditate on that characteristic. Pray about it. Muse on it some. Remember, she who controls her tongue is wise.

The Days of Our Lives

*So teach us to number our days, that we
may present to You a heart of wisdom.*
PSALM 90:12 NASB

The psalmist suggests that we are allotted about "threescore and ten" (70) years (Psalm 90:10 KJV). We sleep and work about 21,000 days. We spend 1,500 days trying to choose what we want to eat. Men spend about 46 days of their lives getting dressed. It takes us women about 136 days doing that same job. Truth is, the days of our lives fly by. The Lord just wants us to number, or literally in Hebrew, "weigh out," those days carefully. Make a calculation. Spend them wisely, starting today.

SOMETIMES HIS PURPOSES ARE HIDDEN

It Is Not for Us to Know

It is not for you to know the times
or the seasons, which the Father
hath put in his own power.
ACTS 1:7 KJV

After Christ's crucifixion, His disciples were huddled together in an upper room afraid for their very lives. They were anxious, and they believed it was a great time to restore Israel to power. In essence they asked, "Are You going to fix it now?" His answer simply put was, "It's not your business to know My timing." In a difficult situation, how often do we ask that same question? Remember, His purpose may be hidden, but it is always revealed at the appropriate time.

Ask for Help

*If you don't know what you're doing, pray to the
Father. He loves to help. You'll get his help, and
won't be condescended to when you ask for it.*
JAMES 1:5 MSG

They told us in school that there are no dumb
questions, but how many times in life have you
asked a question and been made to feel like a
dummy? Well, that will never happen with our
heavenly Father. He wants us to ask. He knows
we are in the dark about a whole lot of things.
He is anxious to help. Just ask.

Unsearchable Things

*"Call to me and I will answer you and
tell you great and unsearchable
things you do not know."*
JEREMIAH 33:3 NIV

We all like to know what's going on. We
spend a lot of time trying to understand the
circumstances of life. We want answers, but
often God promises to give us directions
instead. Jeremiah told us to call upon the
Lord and He would lay out insights into those
"unsearchable" things. Truthfully, those things
may be over our pay grade. We may not
get the entire picture. But when we call, He
answers and guides us along.

He Knows What Is in the Darkness

*"It is He who reveals the profound
and hidden things; He knows
what is in the darkness."*

DANIEL 2:22 NASB

When you were a little girl and the monsters came at night, all you wanted was for your parents to turn on the light. So it is with our heavenly Father. He is the One who knows the end from the beginning. He is aware of the pitfalls of our lives and what lingers in the darkness. He will guide His kids through the unknown stuff. Trust Him to turn the light on.

Pause

Jesus wept.
JOHN 11:35 KJV

When we read the Bible in English, it is easy to miss the nuances of the original language. This well-known passage has some of that hidden importance. There are two words and then a period. But that period is very important. It signifies more than just the end of a sentence. It is an opportunity to pause, to let the message sink in. Jesus cared so much for His friend that He wept (literally, wailed). In our worst predicament, He loves us that much too. Pause, and let that thought sink in.

Protecting Us from Danger

It is the glory of God to conceal a thing.
PROVERBS 25:2 KJV

At first glance, this verse seems to be saying that God loves to play "gotcha." But nothing could be further from the truth. The Hebrew word for *conceal* carries the idea of guarding or protecting someone from some danger. It is a kind of shielding. Since the Lord knows what is coming around the bend, sometimes He conceals it from us as a means of protection. He may not always alert us to what's coming, but He will always go through it with us.

Flexibility Is Required

*Do not boast about tomorrow, for you
do not know what a day may bring forth.*
PROVERBS 27:1 NASB

Although our children believe that because
we have eyes in the back of our head we know
everything, none of us can actually see what's
coming. God's future purposes can be unclear.
So the writer of Proverbs urges us to take
things one day at a time. As we make plans,
we should be open to change. We need to
develop a flexible spirit so God can work in
our lives. Remember, only He can see around
the corner; we are just along for the ride.

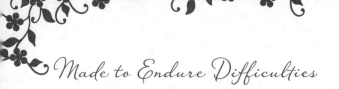

Made to Endure Difficulties

*Immediately Jesus made the disciples
get into the boat and go on ahead
of him to the other side.*

MATTHEW 14:22 NIV

The night Peter walked on water the Bible
says that Jesus made the disciples get into the
boat and head out to sea. The Greek verb for
made means "to constrain or to be forced."
It was God's idea that they launch out, even
though He knew they were in for a rough night
at sea. He didn't prevent their storm, nor will
He always prevent ours. But He does promise
to be with us every step of our journey. Is it
time for you to get out of the boat?

I Am Not Afraid

"Because I, your God, have a firm grip on you and I'm not letting go. I'm telling you, 'Don't panic. I'm right here to help you.'"
ISAIAH 41:13 MSG

After a terrorist attack on a European capital, the people of that city hung a huge banner on one of their fountains. It read, I AM NOT AFRAID. They were not going to cower in fear. Neither should we. If we lose a job or someone is desperately sick, we need to hang a banner on our heart and declare, "I am not afraid. I know who holds my hand. We will go through this together."

A New Thing

*"Do not call to mind the former things,
or ponder things of the past.
Behold, I will do something new."*
ISAIAH 43:18–19 NASB

The very best homemaker gets caught in a rut
with supper menus. And food boredom seeps
into the family dinner hour. The answer is to
try something new. God suggests the same
thing for our spiritual lives. He is ready to
stretch us, to encourage us with new thoughts
and experiences. Our problem is fear of the
unknown. So, maybe today is a great time to
declare, "I am open to new challenges, Lord.
Bring it on!"

Waiting

Wait for the LORD and keep His way.
PSALM 37:34 NASB

When we think of waiting, we are instantly drawn to the idea of a useless waste of time. But in this verse, the psalmist is using a different kind of word for *wait*. In Hebrew, it is the concept of binding something together in order to create strength. There is no useless boredom when we wait on the Lord. It is productive. God is making something strong out of those circumstances, something for our benefit. That kind of waiting is worth waiting for!

His Thoughts Are Not Our Thoughts

"For my thoughts are not your thoughts, neither are your ways my ways."

ISAIAH 55:8 NIV

We were made in God's image (Genesis 1:27), but we are not capable of reasoning as He does. Our minds have limits; His is infinite in scope and creativity. Often His perspective is hidden. So why then do we routinely try to match wits with Almighty God and have our own way? We would be so much better off if we just settled it once and for all. *God, You are in charge. Your ideas are better. Have Your own way, Lord.*

Not Cryptic Anymore

"If you, even you, had only known on this day what would bring you peace— but now it is hidden from your eyes."

LUKE 19:42 NIV

Jesus wept because the Jews didn't understand how to achieve real peace. The Son of God was standing right there, but they didn't get it. His message was "hidden," and He used a Greek term from which we get the word *cryptic*. There was a spiritual encryption, and they didn't have the code. But we do. We have the completed scriptures and can plainly decode the "hidden" message: Christ the Savior has come and brought real peace!

Sometimes It's More Than We Can Bear

"I have much more to say to you, more than you can now bear."

JOHN 16:12 NIV

The night before Jesus allowed Himself to be crucified, He discussed many important spiritual topics with His disciples, including the fact that He was going away. But at a certain point, He acknowledged that some spiritual truth was just too much for them. They couldn't bear it, or understand or deal with the weight of it all. God's plan is sometimes like that. It's just more than we can deal with. So instead of thrashing around, let's choose to trust Him.

Tomorrow

*Don't brashly announce what you're
going to do tomorrow; you don't
know the first thing about tomorrow.*

PROVERBS 27:1 MSG

Most of us order our lives with some kind of a
calendar. But lest we get to believing that we
have it all under control, Solomon reminds us
that our knowledge of the future is extremely
limited. He tells us not to boast about
tomorrow. The Hebrew word literally means
"to shine or shout." It's the idea that we dare
not assume we are in control. But God is, so
let's boast about Him instead.

Know Him, Not His Plan

I want to know Christ.
PHILIPPIANS 3:10 NIV

The English word *know* has a variety of
meanings. But in this scripture it conveys a
specific thought. It implies a kind of seeking or
serious investigation. Paul wants us to examine
Christ carefully—and then apply what we
discover, emulate what we find in His character.
Unfortunately, we spend far too much time
trying to discern His will. We get distracted
in the research. What we really need to do is
spend more time focused on knowing, really
knowing, Him. Discerning His plan will come
later.

IT CAN BE TOUGH

Dance Till It Rains

But as for you, brethren,
do not grow weary of doing good.
2 Thessalonians 3:13 NASB

An aboriginal rainmaker was asked why every time his particular tribe danced, it rained. He answered, "It is very simple, actually; we dance till it rains." They wouldn't stop, no matter what. There is a great lesson for all women in that story. Paul encourages us all to not grow weary while we are doing good. Praying, serving, and loving those around us takes great effort. On occasions, it may be tough and not much fun, but accomplishing God's will is worth it. Keep dancing.

His Grace Is Enough

"My grace is sufficient for you,
for power is perfected in weakness."
2 CORINTHIANS 12:9 NASB

Through every step of life, we all need God's grace. When conflicts arise, finances run short, relationships are ruined, and attitudes are sour, we all need His grace. The wonderful news is that in all circumstances, His grace is enough. Or as Paul wrote, it is sufficient. The Greek word means to be "strong enough" for any task at hand. Doing God's will is hard work. It's a good thing that He provides enough of everything needed for the job!

No Fainting

For which cause we faint not;
but though our outward man perish,
yet the inward man is renewed day by day.
2 Corinthians 4:16 KJV

Stuff happens. Difficulties arise. It's easy to get overwhelmed and spiritually sidetracked. But here Paul urges the Corinthians to not faint, literally, "don't be a coward." Externally things may look bleak, but internally the Spirit of God is at work. And He is refreshing or renewing our spirits every single day. So let's face the day with confidence. No smelling salts necessary.

Help a Friend

*Those of us who are strong and able
in the faith need to step in and lend
a hand to those who falter.*

ROMANS 15:1 MSG

Accomplishing God's plan for our lives takes a group effort. We were never meant to live the life of a Christian in seclusion. When we fall, we need a hand up. We need help from someone who is *strong*. That word means "to be firm, fixed, or established." It is the idea of a seasoned Christian coming alongside and helping a rookie in the faith. Do you need help today, or can you help someone else?

Run with Endurance

*Let us run with endurance the race that is
set before us, fixing our eyes on Jesus.*
HEBREWS 12:1–2 NASB

To run the race of life with endurance is
difficult. Paul gives us a great word picture
for that concept of perseverance. It is a
compound Greek word that conveys the idea
of remaining under something and waiting
with an expectant heart. There is a strain, but
we stay bent over, supporting the weight.
That's how we engage life when God's plan
seems too tough. We endure or stay in
position and wait with hope.

He Will Restore Us

He restoreth my soul.
PSALM 23:3 KJV

This is a song about sheep, and they are very stupid animals. That's why the shepherd had to be with them at all times. If a sheep got into a thicket and rolled over on its back, it could not right itself. Left there unattended, it wouldn't take long for the gases in the sheep's stomach to build up and literally choke it to death. The sheep would need to be restored, stood upright, and reset into a healthy position. We are so like sheep—how do you need to be restored today?

Hemmed in with Troubles

*We continue to shout our praise even
when we're hemmed in with troubles.*
ROMANS 5:3 MSG

Paul isn't a masochist. He has a reason for
encouraging us to see our troubles in a
positive light. He connects trials with the
acquisition of patience, and he notes that
patience produces character. Remembering
those previous difficult moments and how
God protected us can encourage our walk. So
today, based on those previous experiences
with the Lord, let's face our difficulties with an
expectant heart and shout out some praises.

But God

*My flesh and my heart may fail,
but God is the strength of my
heart and my portion forever.*

PSALM 73:26 NASB

Trying to pursue God's purpose for our lives is tough. We often stumble and fall. We get distracted. The psalmist knew that we might easily get discouraged, so he inserted the phrase "but God." He was reminding us that when we are weak, God is strong. When we fail, He steps in. And ultimately He becomes our portion forever. The Hebrew word for portion refers to a part of a plunder or prize. In the end, He is what we win.

Who Wins?

For I do not do the good I want to do,
but the evil I do not want to do—
this I keep on doing.

ROMANS 7:19 NIV

There is a story about two wolves. One was evil and the other a good wolf filled with kindness and forgiveness. They fight, and the question is, who wins? A wise old Indian grandfather observed, "The one we feed." There are two natures inside every Christian as well. A war rages, and the same question applies: Who wins? Let's feed the new nature today with scripture, spiritual songs, and prayer.

Hyper Nikes

No, in all these things we are more than conquerors through him who loved us.
ROMANS 8:37 NIV

In Greek, "more than conquerors" is a single compound Greek term. *Huper* is the Greek way of saying "more," and *nikao* (transliterated NIKE by the shoe company) means "to conquer or overcome." When you put it together, you get the idea of a super conqueror. In colloquial terms, we are not run-of-the-mill conquerors. We are all Hyper Nikes! And in the immediate context, we can conquer death, life, angels, principalities, powers, and things to come.

Everyone Needs Some Rest

Rest in the LORD,
and wait patiently for him.
PSALM 37:7 KJV

A small glass of water weighs about eight ounces. Holding it in your hand for a few seconds would be no big deal. Holding it for an hour, your arm might ache. But if you hold it for an entire day, you may need a doctor. Any burden held incessantly is too much to handle. In this song, David outlines a balanced way of life. He starts by telling us not to fret but to trust. He urges us to delight in the Lord as we commit our ways to Him. And ultimately that process will result in rest for our souls. Ahhhhh.

Blessings in Disguise

Consider it pure joy, my brothers and sisters,
whenever you face trials of many kinds.
JAMES 1:2 NIV

Laura Story has a great song entitled
"Blessings." She asks some key questions:
"What if blessings come through raindrops?
What if your healing comes through tears?
What if the trials of this life are Your mercies
in disguise?" And the answer is, we need
to consider those difficulties a form of joy.
We need to intentionally reset our attitudes
(regardless of the circumstances) and trust our
heavenly Father. But it is okay to say, "Daddy,
it's dark in here; hold my hand."

911 Phone Call

*I call on the L*ORD *in my distress,*
and he answers me.
PSALM 120:1 NIV

Women make emergency phone calls for all kinds of reasons. Kids get their heads stuck in toilets, moms get their hands wedged in blenders, or there are more serious accidents. In this verse, the Hebrew word for *distress* carries the idea of an extreme discomfort, an anguish, or a serious affliction. And the psalmist tells us how to make the correct emergency call. When our world crashes, we need to call the One who can help, our heavenly Father. Dial Him today.

Hurdles

*"Be strong and courageous, and do the work.
Do not be afraid or discouraged."*
1 CHRONICLES 28:20 NIV

Running around life's track is a piece of cake
until someone sets up those two-foot barriers
we call hurdles. And suddenly "doing the
work" gets very difficult. Our hurdles can take
on the form of an empty checkbook, or a nasty
confrontation with a rebellious teenager, or a
strained conversation with our husband. We
need to learn to attack those hurdles with
courageous faith. It may not be pretty for a
while, but with practice and patience, we can
learn to soar over them.

I Will Make You Recover

Come unto me, all ye that labour and
are heavy laden, and I will give you rest.
MATTHEW 11:28 KJV

The invitation is to the weary (literally, those who are cut or who have pain) and the heavy laden (those with a burden loaded on by others). And Jesus promises rest. But the Greek translation carries a much more dynamic message than just "I will give you rest." It says, "I will rest you, I will make you recover." We come all beat up, and Jesus will force us to be healed. No arguing, we will be made to rest!

PREPPING TO DO HIS WILL

Kindness Takes Work

*And be ye kind one to another,
tenderhearted, forgiving one another.*
EPHESIANS 4:32 KJV

In the Old Testament, Eliezer was asked to find a wife for his master, Isaac. He stopped by a well and interviewed some possible candidates by asking them for some water for his camels. Rebekah watered all ten camels. A camel will drink between nine and twenty gallons a day. A gallon of water weighs eight pounds. She lifted up to 1,600 pounds of water as a simple act of kindness. What kind thing could you do today?

A Message of Resolve

*"But even if he does not. . .
we will not serve your gods."*
DANIEL 3:18 NIV

In 1940 the Allied troops were trapped on the beaches of Dunkirk. Stuck in a dire situation, they sent a terse message back across the Channel. It read: "And if not. . ." It wasn't some sort of code; it referenced the message the three Hebrew children gave Nebuchadnezzar in an equally threatening moment. It was a statement of resolve. Even if God doesn't rescue us in the manner we might wish, we will still serve Him. Do you have your back up against a wall today? You can join in the chorus, "Even if He doesn't. . ."

Keeping Humble

"He must increase,
but I must decrease."
JOHN 3:30 NASB

Accomplishing God's purposes in our lives requires preparation and attitude adjustments. On a daily basis, we need a mind-set of humility. In ancient Rome, a slave was assigned to stand next to a conquering hero and regularly whisper *memento mori*—"remember your mortality." There is a practical implication of that Latin phrase for modern women. Remembering we are mortal can help us remain humble. Christ and His influence must increase, our importance must decrease. Do you need to remind a friend, "Memento mori"?

Spiritual Landmarks

*Do not move the ancient boundary
which your fathers have set.*
PROVERBS 22:28 NASB

The Israelites marked their property with
stones at the corners of the fields. These
ancient landmarks were not to be moved.
They helped provide structure to their society.
Our spiritual landmarks do the same thing.
Our baptism marks our public declaration of
faith. Our attendance at church says Jesus
is a focus of our week. And when we open
our Bibles, we are displaying a landmark of
sorts. We are declaring, "Christ matters to me
every single day." So don't move your ancient
landmarks; they matter.

No More Barns

*And he said, This will I do: I will pull
down my barns, and build greater.*
LUKE 12:18 KJV

Part of being prepared to accomplish God's
will for our lives involves simplification. Our
tendency is to do the exact opposite. The rich
ruler stated as much in this verse. "I have more
stuff; I will build more barns." Wrong. We need
to clean out, clear out, and prioritize. No more
barns. We need to learn the secret of being
content with what we do have, not yearning
for more.

The Need for Quiet Prayer

But Jesus often withdrew to lonely places and prayed.

LUKE 5:16 NIV

Other translations render "lonely places" as "wilderness." As the multitudes pressed in on Jesus, He sought out a remote, desolate region where He could be alone with His Father. He knew that His Spirit needed to be refreshed, and only spending uninterrupted time with God the Father would meet that need. So it is with us. Our wilderness might be a basement or a closet or the backseat of a van, but we too need time for quiet prayer. Seek it out today.

Fix Your Attention on Jesus

Don't become so well-adjusted to your culture
that you fit into it without even thinking.
Instead, fix your attention on God.

ROMANS 12:2 MSG

Paul is urging the church in Rome (and us) to
stop being molded by the external routines
of their culture and instead to be transformed
by an inner change, a change brought on by
a consistent redirecting of their minds. That's
great counsel for today. Simply put, fix your
attention on Jesus. As the old hymn says:
"Look full in His wonderful face and the things
of earth will grow strangely dim. . . ."

Deny Yourself

*"Whoever wants to be my disciple
must deny themselves and take
up their cross and follow me."*

MARK 8:34 NIV

As disciples of Jesus, we have a distinct purpose in life. In order to focus on that purpose, Mark tells us to deny ourselves. Biblically, that phrase means to virtually disown yourself. It is the idea of quashing or crushing your own interests in light of someone else's priority. When Christ takes first place in our lives, we begin to systematically reprioritize our interests. "Him first" becomes the cry. What should you start reprioritizing today?

Confession

*If we confess our sins, he is faithful
and just to forgive us our sins.*
1 JOHN 1:9 KJV

In the original language, *confess* means "to
say the same thing about something." In
other words, we are supposed to say the same
thing about our sin that God says about it.
We can't use excuses like, "Well, it was just
an exaggeration." Instead, we have to call it
what He does: "That was a lie. I did not tell
the truth." When we confess with that kind of
clarity, He is definitely faithful to forgive us.
What's on your sin list today?

A New Wardrobe

You're done with that old life. It's like a filthy set of ill-fitting clothes you've stripped off and put in the fire. Now you're dressed in a new wardrobe.
COLOSSIANS 3:9–10 MSG

Every woman loves to replenish her wardrobe. We are thrilled to throw out the old stuff and select a new outfit. Using that analogy, Paul describes a new reality for the believer. He says we are done with the old life; we have stripped off the old. We are not bound by our old sinful habits. We are made new. Let's appreciate our new spiritual outfits!

Be Ready to Give an Answer

Keep your hearts at attention, in adoration before Christ, your Master. Be ready to speak up and tell anyone who asks why you're living the way you are.

1 PETER 3:15 MSG

The number one phobia in America is glossophobia, the fear of public speaking. And yet that is exactly what Peter was telling his audience to do. In the original language, he's saying be prepared to give a speech or explanation of your faith. When someone wants to know why we live like we do, we must be prepared with a clear and concise answer. Do you have one ready?

Check Out the Ant

Go to the ant, O sluggard,
observe her ways and be wise.
PROVERBS 6:6 NASB

Solomon, the wisest man on earth, spent some time down on his hands and knees observing the lowly ant. He noticed that the ant prepares its food well in advance and therefore has something to harvest down the road. He urges his readers to make a similar connection. Earthly preparation is important; spiritual preparation is also important. What should we be doing today to store up some encouragement for tomorrow? Memorizing scripture is a good start.

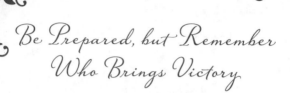

Be Prepared, but Remember Who Brings Victory

The horse is prepared for the day of battle,
but victory belongs to the Lord.
PROVERBS 21:31 NASB

Stockpiling what's needed for a battle is an important part of a winning strategy. If we lived during the time when men fought on horseback, we would understand the value of armor and prepping horses properly for a skirmish. But we would soon learn that armor alone does not ensure success. The victory comes from the Lord. We still need to get spiritually prepped for our everyday struggles, but ultimately our confidence dare not be in that effort alone. Our trust is in Him.

Discipline Is a Good Thing

Blessed is the one you discipline, LORD.
PSALM 94:12 NIV

Perspective is everything in life. And here the biblical songwriter inserts an amazing thought. In Hebrew he says, "O the bliss of discipline!" Or he might have said, "Happy is the woman who is chastened by the Lord." It is a godly perspective to be able to see the benefit of a spiritual spanking. It means first of all that God loves us enough to care how we behave. And He loves us enough to correct us so that we can become more like His Son. "O the bliss. . ."

Our Stride

In their hearts humans plan their course,
but the Lord establishes their steps.
PROVERBS 16:9 NIV

Many women wear a fitness device that counts their steps every day. But what we really need is a spiritual scanner. In this verse, the Hebrew noun translated "course" conveys the idea of a path that is selected. But the term for "steps" implies the actual stride, or the distance that is covered. We might choose a course of action in life, but God determines the successful accomplishment of His will. We might select the general direction to take, but remember, stride for stride He controls the outcome.

USEFUL AT ANY AGE

Serving Him in Our Youth

And don't let anyone put you down because you're young. Teach believers with your life.
1 TIMOTHY 4:12 MSG

Living out God's purposes for our lives has absolutely nothing to do with our age or stage of life. Paul respected his young protégé a great deal. He saw significant value and worth in Timothy's life and ministry. He urged him to "stay at your post" (1 Timothy 4:13 MSG) and ignore the comments of others. Teenagers and young adults have a unique energy available for the cause of Christ. So let's use it for the greater good!

Gray Hair

A gray head is a crown of glory.
PROVERBS 16:31 NASB

Over the course of her lifetime, a woman may spend more than $20,000 coloring her gray hair. And that's if they do the job themselves. Clearly, the message that gray hair is a mark of distinction has been lost on many of us. In this verse, God is endorsing the wisdom to be gained through the ups and downs of everyday life. And there is a reward for those who do it well. Take a look in the mirror today and marvel at the crown of glory God has given you. Leave it gray!

New Goals

"Now then, give me this hill country."
JOSHUA 14:12 NASB

Joshua was eighty-five years old when he asked Moses for this new challenge. His enthusiasm brings to mind a missionary to India named Evelyn Brand. She was fifty years old when her husband died. Against the recommendation of her mission's board, she stayed in the hill country ministering for another twenty years. When she fell off her pony and broke her hip, she still didn't head home. The grateful villagers carried her up and down the mountain until she died at ninety-five. Age doesn't determine our usefulness; our determination does.

Strength as We Age

Strengthen the feeble hands, steady the knees that give way; say to those with fearful hearts, "Be strong, do not fear."
ISAIAH 35:3–4 NIV

Most women spend an inordinate amount of time, interest, and money trying desperately to ignore the signs of aging. But the truth is, our bones creak a bit and we squint to read; maybe we walk with a limp and fall asleep before the good stuff comes on TV. We need physical strength to meet the challenges of growing older. And God promises to provide just that.

The Good Old Days

Do not say, "Why were the old days better than these?" For it is not wise to ask such questions.

ECCLESIASTES 7:10 NIV

Were the "good old days" really better than today? Or do we just have selective memories? Were the kids cuter at three than six? Was the house quieter before teenagers? The truth is, there was yesterday, and it is different from today. There was the day before yesterday, and it was different still. Instead of longing for a time that is behind us, let's embrace the good of today.

Growing in Grace

But grow in the grace and knowledge
of our Lord and Savior Jesus Christ.
2 PETER 3:18 NASB

In C. S. Lewis's book *Prince Caspian*, Lucy
remarks, " 'Aslan [the lion who represents God],
you're bigger.' 'That is because you are older,
little one,' answered he. 'Not because you are?'
'I am not. But every year you grow, you will
find me bigger.' " That's why Peter urges us all
to grow in grace. In every season of spiritual
growth, God seems to occupy a bit more space
in our lives. He "grows" as we grow. How are
you growing today?

Suffering in Old Age

So then, those who suffer according to God's will should commit themselves to their faithful Creator and continue to do good.

1 Peter 4:19 NIV

Those who are a bit over sixty might like to paraphrase a well-known hymn with these words: "It is well with my soul, but my knees hurt." There is no doubt that with age come aches and pains of all kinds, some more serious than others. Regardless of the intensity of the discomfort, our focus ought to be: continue to do good. It might take an attitude change, but it's worth it!

Caring for the Elderly

Any Christian woman who has widows
in her family is responsible for them.
They shouldn't be dumped on the church.

1 Timothy 5:16 MSG

Every year in the United States, 700,000 women lose their husbands, and those women will then remain widows for an average of fourteen years. They all have needs, from simple things like a ride to church to more significant issues like financial assistance. Paul was establishing a priority for women to help other women. It's a duty, not an option. Is there someone in your life who needs your help? Reach out today.

Don't Say I Am Too Young

Then said I, Ah, Lord GOD! behold,
I cannot speak: for I am a child.

JEREMIAH 1:6 KJV

Jeremiah tried hard to disqualify himself from spiritual service. First he declares, "I am too young." And then he uses the same phrase that Moses used to refer to his own speaking ability: "I am not eloquent." But the Lord doesn't care if he is young and lacks the gift of public speaking. God has a job for this young prophet, and He expects him to get it done. Age and skill sets are not the prerequisites for service; faithfulness is.

Confident Since Childhood

For you have been my hope, Sovereign LORD,
my confidence since my youth.

PSALM 71:5 NIV

This ancient songwriter is making some bold
statements about his walk with the Lord.
Looking back on his childhood, he is declaring
that God has been the source of his safety and
security for as long as he can remember. He
uses a Hebrew word that spotlights a kind of
absolute trust, and he focuses it on Yahweh.
That's great insight for a young boy. Prayerfully
we too can say the same thing about where
our confidence lies.

The Behavior of Older Women

The aged women likewise, that they be
in behaviour as becometh holiness.

TITUS 2:3 KJV

In this passage, Paul is giving a litany of
behavioral instructions for the people of God.
He calls out character qualities for both older
and younger men and women. To the older
women, he focuses in on their behavior or,
literally, their position in society. They are
exhorted to live a life that is holy or sacred.
They are honorable. Their godliness was to set
them apart. Does ours?

Life Is Short

For what is your life? It is even a vapour,
that appeareth for a little time,
and then vanisheth away.

JAMES 4:14 KJV

Regardless of our age, it's helpful to remember
that life is short. James compares life to
a vapor and uses a term that refers to the
exhalation of our breath. It is useful while it's
in our body, but then it's exhaled and gone.
Life is meant to be full and vibrant, but once
it's gone, its usefulness is finished. So let's
cherish these moments: hug our kids, love
our husbands, care for your parents, and
encourage our coworkers. Do things that
matter.

A Long Life

"Honor your father and your mother,
so that you may live long in the land
the LORD your God is giving you."
EXODUS 20:12 NIV

This is one of the Ten Commandments, and it has a promise attached to it. Repeated again in the book of Ephesians, it connects the life expectancy of children with their relationship to their parents. We don't stop being a daughter when we become a mother. Respect and appreciation for our parents must continue regardless of our season of life. Want a few more years? Deal graciously with your parents.

Starting off Right

Train up a child in the way he should go:
and when he is old, he will not depart from it.
PROVERBS 22:6 KJV

Many moms look at this verse as a kind of
guarantee. If we have our kids in church every
week and control the media in the house,
then they will turn out right. But the verb for
train here literally means "to create a thirst."
It's our job to set a spiritual environment in
our home where Christ is the natural center
of everything. Then, they learn to crave after
Him. Then, they will not depart from it.

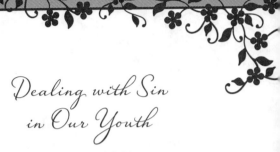

Dealing with Sin in Our Youth

Flee also youthful lusts.
2 Timothy 2:22 KJV

In each season of life, there are particular sins that "easily beset us" (Hebrews 12:1 KJV). But teenagers seem to have a particular boatload of challenges and temptations. Here, Paul gave Timothy insight into how to deal with youthful lust. He told him to flee or, more specifically, run! At any age, the secret to dealing with a tough temptation is to run away quickly. No pausing, no conversations, no sharing, no dabbling—just run! Got your running shoes on today?

Young, Untested

David the king addressed the congregation: "My son Solomon was singled out and chosen by God to do this. But he's young and untested."

1 CHRONICLES 29:1 MSG

David knew building the temple was a mammoth undertaking. He knew his son was young and inexperienced, but he also knew that God had chosen him for that assignment. Too often we focus on the training of an individual, their experience, their skill set, before we entrust them with a responsibility. God's plan is the opposite. He calls, then He equips. Regardless of your age, have you been given a task? Get it done.

A Good Old Age

"You shall go to your fathers in peace;
you will be buried at a good old age."

GENESIS 15:15 NASB

Based on the way we keep looking for the fountain of youth, most of us want to ignore the whole topic of death. Not Abraham, for he was going to die in peace and be buried at "a good old age." In Hebrew, this term implies a time that is appealing or pleasant to the senses, a time that is proper or even convenient. It's the right time. Because of Christ, we too will be buried at "a good old age." We have nothing to fear!

HIS WORD
LEADS THE WAY

A Path to Follow

*I am the LORD thy God. . .which leadeth
thee by the way that thou shouldest go.*
ISAIAH 48:17 KJV

The Hebrew word for *lead* in this verse literally
means "to tread or bend." It is the idea that
on a nature walk you might step in front of
the kids and clear a path. You lead them by
trampling down the obstacles. When we seek
out the Lord in His Word, He does exactly the
same thing for us. He leads us by stomping
down the barriers that block our spiritual
progress. Spend some time with Him today.

Eager Hearts

For they received the word with great eagerness, examining the Scriptures daily.
ACTS 17:11 NASB

An excellent dinner starts with a good recipe. A great hike in the woods begins with a current map. And no one would dream of sewing a dress without a detailed pattern. We all need directions. And we are doomed to a life of spiritual mediocrity if we do not immerse ourselves into God's Word every single day. His plan for our lives is unfolded as we read and study the Bible. We don't need a theology degree; we just need an eager heart.

Clean

*Now ye are clean through the word
which I have spoken unto you.*

JOHN 15:3 KJV

Every homemaker knows what it is to clean
something. So we understand the principle
that Christ shed His blood to cleanse us from
all unrighteousness. In this verse, John uses
a particular word for *clean*. It is a Greek word
from which we get the term *catharsis*. This
clean is more than the act of just scrubbing; it
is the process of getting relief from something.
So take a big breath as you read His Word
today, and relish the relief from the shame
associated with our sin.

His Word Is Always Productive

"So will the words that come out of my mouth not come back empty-handed. They'll do the work I sent them to do."

ISAIAH 55:11 MSG

The instructions and encouragements that come from God's Word are sent on purpose. The Holy Spirit directs them, and those words will accomplish the job God sends them to do. Some days they convict, and we must respond. Some days they direct, and we must go. Every day they are purposeful in our lives. God won't allow His Word to be unproductive.

Spiritual Flashlights

*Your word is a lamp for my feet,
a light on my path.*
PSALM 119:105 NIV

There are penlights, rechargeable flashlights, lanterns, headlights, and colorful nightsticks. All of them are designed to light up the area where you are walking and help you avoid an accident. God's Word is just such a light for our lives. The everyday paths that we trudge down need illumination. We need to know which direction to choose and which danger to avoid. Grab your Bible and shed some light on your day.

Worthless Stuff

*Turn my eyes away from worthless things;
preserve my life according to your word.*
PSALM 119:37 NIV

Women watch almost 166 hours of TV per
month, 16 hours more than men. And yet,
many of us say we do not have time to spend
in God's Word. The truth is, the book of
Malachi would take about 8 minutes to read.
We could consume the entire book of Genesis
in about 3 hours and 45 minutes. Staying true
to God's purposes requires time in His Book.
Let's start turning our eyes away from the
worthless stuff and spend time with our Savior.

Valuable Benefits

For the LORD *gives wisdom.*
PROVERBS 2:6 NIV

Every now and again, American Express sends out nice glossy postcards to announce valuable new benefits. With each announcement, they want cardholders to feel better. They want us shoppers to know that now we have more access or more purchasing power or more travel options, or more everything. Well, if they can do that with a credit card, imagine what it would be like if we regularly received creative, well-written, enticing announcements about something really important. Oh yeah, we do! Let's open our Bibles and check out the valuable benefits!

Cherishing God's Word

Thy law is my delight.
PSALM 119:174 KJV

One of the artifacts recovered from New York's
Ground Zero was a hunk of metal with a bunch
of Bible pages fused to it. Someone had their
Bible with them in the World Trade Center that
fateful day. It must have been their delight.
That's what the psalmist calls God's Word
in Psalm 119. In that chapter, he uses eight
different terms for God's law. He calls it the
Torah, the Word, the statutes, the commands,
the decrees, the precepts, the promise, and
the laws. Regardless of the term used, it was
his delight. Do you cherish your Bible?

Stuffing Our Faces

Your words were found and I ate them,
and Your words became for me a joy.
JEREMIAH 15:16 NASB

There is a petite mother in Texas who holds a world record for consuming two 72-ounce steaks along with a baked potato, a roll, some shrimp cocktail, and a salad all in less than fifteen minutes! Women love to eat. But instead of stuffing our faces with favorite foods, let's mirror the sentiment of the prophet Jeremiah. He "ate" the words of the Lord, and they filled his heart with joy. That kind of a meal can really satisfy our hearts. Bon appétit!

God's Word Accomplishes Its Purpose

*"So will the words that come out of my
mouth not come back empty-handed.
They'll do the work I sent them to do,
they'll complete the assignment I gave them."*

ISAIAH 55:11 MSG

As we seek to accomplish God's plan for
our lives, we can follow the scriptures with
confidence. In this verse, He is stating that His
words do not return empty-handed or void.
When needed, His Word directs, encourages,
convicts, or calms. It highlights mercy and
promises justice. We can take it to the bank.
His Word accomplishes His purposes. Let's
turn it loose in our lives.

The Source of Wisdom

*"The breath of the Almighty
gives them understanding."*
JOB 32:8 NASB

Some folks like to use tea leaves or tarot cards or charts of the stars to help guide their decisions in life. But Job's friend Elihu makes it clear in this passage that insight and understanding come directly from God. He uses the expression "breath of the Almighty" to make sure we know that the source of all wisdom is the mind of the Lord. Our marching orders come directly from Him and should be followed. Let's skip the silly stuff and open His Word.

Fear Him

*"Oh that they had such a heart in them,
that they would fear Me and keep all
My commandments always."*

DEUTERONOMY 5:29 NASB

We live in a very permissive society, and almost no mother wants her child to fear her. But God does. He wants His kids to have a kind of reverential awe associated with serving Him. He wants our respect and the honor that He is due. Perhaps if we concentrated a bit more on His transcendence (the ways in which He is not like us at all), we might get Him back on the throne of our hearts where He belongs.

Great Eagerness

For they received the word with great eagerness,
examining the Scriptures daily.
ACTS 17:11 NASB

What kinds of things do you look forward
to with great eagerness? Making a great
meal for your family? Planning a well-
deserved vacation? Well, in this verse, Paul
is commending the church at Berea for their
eagerness to dive into the scriptures every
single day. *Eagerness* in Greek means to
be ready, to have "clarity of mind." He is
commending them for the daily discipline it
takes to be in God's Word. We can't follow
His plan if we don't study His Word with
eagerness!

Banking Your Promises

*I've banked your promises in the vault of
my heart so I won't sin myself bankrupt.*

PSALM 119:11 MSG

One of the ways we know we have real
purpose in life is to check the promises of God
we have hidden away in our hearts. When the
psalmist penned this song, he used a Hebrew
word for *hid* or *bank* that literally means "to
conceal something of great value." As we
store up His promises, we are building a
hedge against fear and the sins that seem to
so easily entangle us. What a deposit! What a
return on investment!

His Instructions

I gain understanding from your precepts;
therefore I hate every wrong path.
PSALM 119:104 NIV

The psalmist used the Hebrew word for *precepts* twenty-one times in this particular song. It is always in the plural form, and it carries the idea of instruction. We are told to seek God's instructions, keep them, and make sure we don't forget them. God is making clear how He wants things done. Our job is to immerse ourselves in His Word so that we can avoid the discipline associated with wrong choices. Is there a particular instruction you need to follow today?

PEACE COMES

Submission

*"Submit to God and
be at peace with him."*
JOB 22:21 NIV

Other translations of this verse suggest that
we should "yield" or "acquaint ourselves"
with God, and then we can be at peace with
Him. The idea is to be so familiar with Him
and His ways that getting in step is easy.
When we understand His directions and go
with the flow, our burdens are lifted and our
attitudes are encouraged. Listen carefully,
you can almost hear Him calling cadence as
we march along. Let the peace settle in.

His Peace Protects

*And the peace of God, which passeth
all understanding, shall keep your hearts
and minds through Christ Jesus.*

PHILIPPIANS 4:7 KJV

Paul uses a strong word to describe how God's
peace can protect our emotions. Our minds
are not just being kept; they are guarded.
Imagine two huge soldiers standing post
outside each of our hearts. When worry and
anxiety begin to monopolize our emotions,
we need help. We need to call on the guards.
And the peace of God will invade our souls,
putting our hearts at rest.

He Wants In

*"I stand at the door and knock. If anyone
hears my voice and opens the door,
I will come in and eat with that person."*
REVELATION 3:20 NIV

While we often use this verse as an evangelistic
tool, in context it was directed to the Church.
The verb tense suggests that Christ has
been standing at the door of our hearts for a
long time and He continues to knock. He is
persistent. Bottom line, He wants to be with
us. So let's just do the obvious thing. Open the
door and make Him a part of our day today.

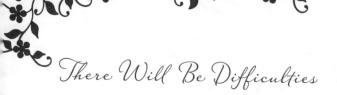

There Will Be Difficulties

*"In this godless world you will continue
to experience difficulties. But take heart!
I've conquered the world."*
JOHN 16:33 MSG

Most of us want to believe that pursuing God's purpose for our lives automatically earns us a "get out of jail free" card. No more problems for us! But that isn't how it works. Instead, Christ promises to conquer those difficulties. Literally, He promises to subdue or overcome them and render us victorious in spite of the anguish. He stands with us in the midst of the junk. Good deal!

His Parting Gift

"That's my parting gift to you. Peace. I don't leave you the way you're used to being left—feeling abandoned, bereft. So don't be upset."

JOHN 14:27 MSG

The most significant gift anyone could ever be given is the peace of God. The night before He died, Christ made sure His disciples understood that truth. He promised to never leave them alone. He promised to be with them in all circumstances. And He promised them a gift, a confident assurance that could structure and give meaning to their entire life. He promised them (and us) His peace. Are you leaning into it today?

Our Mind-Set

For the mind set on the flesh is death, but the mind set on the Spirit is life and peace.

ROMANS 8:6 NASB

In Christ, we have dignity and worth. We have significant purpose in life, but pursuing that purpose on a daily basis is a challenge. So Paul reminded the church in Rome to have their minds (hearts and wills) bent or set toward the Lord. We need a default button set on Him. When the inclinations of our thoughts are toward Him, and not focused on us, the result is a sense of real peace.

Sustained

"The steadfast of mind You will keep in perfect peace, because he trusts in You."
ISAIAH 26:3 NASB

When the pressures and stresses of everyday living invade our souls, anxiety is the result. Our focus becomes misplaced on the difficulties at hand, and our ability to concentrate is frayed. We crave clarity. And when we place our trust in the Lord, He promises to provide just such a focus. He calls it a "perfect" (or complete or safe) peace. It's enough. It will sustain us. Try it.

Great Peace

Great peace have they which love thy law:
and nothing shall offend them.

PSALM 119:165 KJV

God's gift of peace is not a trinket. When our minds and hearts are still and focused on His Word, great peace is the gift. This adjective conveys abundance, something long or mighty. It's not an ordinary emotion; it's an extraordinary assurance. With that kind of peace, nothing can offend or cause us to stumble. Our hearts are full and sustained. Regardless of the challenge, we have great peace for today.

At All Times and in Every Way

Now may the Lord of peace himself give
you peace at all times and in every way.
2 THESSALONIANS 3:16 NIV

It is human nature to try and find loopholes in agreements. When we read this verse, we might be tempted to try and think of an exception when the Lord might not provide His peace in a given situation. But just to make sure we walk through life and pursue His purposes with complete assurance, Paul uses terms like "at all times" and "in every way." Peace for every situation we may face. Wow.

The Price for Our Peace

But he was pierced for our transgressions,
he was crushed for our iniquities;
the punishment that brought us
peace was on him.

Isaiah 53:5 NIV

A holy and righteous God cannot ignore the evil associated with sin. It must be dealt with; there is a punishment that must be exacted. That payment was paid in full on the cross as Jesus cried, "It is finished." The peace that today floods each of our souls was expensive. It cost Christ His life. Let's cherish it today.

Peaceful Sleep

I will both lay me down in peace,
and sleep: for thou, LORD,
only makest me dwell in safety.

PSALM 4:8 KJV

Insomnia is a huge problem for women. And
the usual remedies of avoiding caffeine,
following a set routine for bedtime, and
keeping our rooms dark and cool may not
solve the problem. When we are stirred with
fears and frustrations, only the Lord can clear
a path to restful, rejuvenating sleep. He does
so by making us rest in safety. He is awake and
providing our security; we get peaceful sleep.
Take Him up on it tonight!

Announcing Good News

*How lovely on the mountains are the feet
of him who brings good news, who announces
peace and brings good news of happiness.*

Isaiah 52:7 NASB

Once we have embraced the message of
the Gospel, it's our turn to go and become
publishers of peace. If we had the cure for
cancer, we would not keep it to ourselves.
Since the truth of the Gospel is so much more
important, let's start sharing good news. Is
there someone struggling at work? Does
a friend need forgiveness? Is a neighbor
alone with their fears? Let's go tell it on the
mountain—real peace is available!

Fruit of the Spirit

But what happens when we live God's way? He brings gifts into our lives, much the same way that fruit appears in an orchard—things like affection for others, exuberance about life, serenity.
GALATIANS 5:22 MSG

The Lord orders the life of a believer. He has a plan for us. And when we live out that plan, He rewards us with a spiritual harvest. He calls that the fruit of the Spirit. Personal peace is part of that fruit. But remember, that peace or serenity is hinged on obedience. We need to keep saying yes to the Lord every single day.

Shalom

I will listen to what God the LORD says;
he promises peace to his people.
PSALM 85:8 NIV

In the Old Testament, the Hebrew word for peace is *shalom*. Peace can exist between people, nations, and God and His people. The foundation of that peace is a covenant or kind of promise. In this verse, God makes sure we understand that His peace is the result of Him keeping a promise. It is not the result of our work. Our job is to listen to what He says. Are you experiencing shalom right now? Are you listening to Him?

Filled Up

*May the God of hope fill you with all
joy and peace as you trust in him.*

ROMANS 15:13 NIV

After Thanksgiving dinner, everyone's stomach
is filled up to the brim with delicious food. We
might say, "We are stuffed." In a similar way,
when we as believers put our regular, everyday
trust in the Savior, we are stuffed or "filled
up" with joy and peace. Pursuing the will of
God and working at His plan for our lives is
a full-time pursuit. But it has amazing results!
Today God wants you to know that you have
purpose, and pursuing it will bring real, lasting
peace.

LOOKING FOR MORE
ENCOURAGEMENT FOR YOUR HEART?

Today God Wants You to Know. . .You Are Beautiful
Paperback / 978-1-68322-257-6 / $4.99

Today God Wants You to Know. . .You Are Blessed
Paperback / 978-1-68322-590-4 / $4.99

Today God Wants You to Know. . .You Are Loved
Paperback / 978-1-64352-154-1 / $4.99

Within the pages of these charming women's devotionals, you'll find the encouragement you need to celebrate every day, as you are reminded that you are a beloved daughter of the King. With more than 180 just-right-sized readings, each encouraging devotional is accompanied by a related scripture selection that will leave you feeling perfectly loved, blessed, and cherished by your heavenly Father.